The Library of Small Ecosystems™

The Ecosystem of a
Garden

Elaine Pascoe   Photography by **Dwight Kuhn**

The Rosen Publishing Group's
PowerKids Press™
New York

Published in 2003 by The Rosen Publishing Group, Inc.
29 East 21st Street, New York, NY 10010

First Edition

Editor: Nancy MacDonell Smith
Book Design: Michael J. Caroleo
Page Layout: Colin Dizengoff, Nick Sciacca

Photo Credits: Photos © Dwight Kuhn.

Pascoe, Elaine.
The ecosystem of a garden / by Elaine Pascoe.— 1st ed.
     p. cm. — (The library of small ecosystems)
Includes bibliographical references (p.   ).
Summary: Simple text explores how insects, birds, and other animals find food and make their homes among the plants of a garden.
ISBN 0-8239-6306-3 (lib. bdg.)
1. Garden ecology—Juvenile literature. [1. Garden ecology. 2. Ecology.] I. Title.
QH541.5.G37 P37 2003
577.5'54—dc21

                         2001006017

Manufactured in the United States of America

Contents

The Garden

Gardens are not wild. People plant them. Yet you can find many kinds of wildlife in a garden.

A garden is the center of a small **ecosystem**, a community of living and nonliving things. Many kinds of plants grow in a garden. Insects, birds, and other animals find food and make their homes among the plants. They are all members of the garden community. Even the soil in which the plants grow is part of the ecosystem. Every part of the ecosystem is important.

From the birds that use the birdbath to the grass underfoot, a garden is a very busy place.

Flowers and More

All kinds of colorful flowers bloom from spring through fall in a garden. In a fruit and vegetable patch, tomatoes, berries, and other plants ripen slowly during the summer. Trees and grass grow around the edges of a garden. Weeds often grow in a garden. Weeds are wild plants that take root in the rich soil. Gardeners don't like _____ they use up **nutrients** in the soil t_____ants.

With so many dif_____ garden has a lot to offer in_____ that come looking for food. A_____own on the ground, the garde_____

The colors and scents of flowers attract bees and other insects to a garden.

Garden vegetables such as these tomatoes attract many different kinds of wildlife.

This colorful beetle, called a sugar-maple borer, feeds on the nectar in a garden flower.

A toad hunts for insects in a garden's lettuce patch.

Garden Insects

For insects, a summer garden is an all-you-can-eat **buffet**. Some insects feed on leaves and other plant parts. Bees and butterflies feed on **nectar**, a sweet liquid in the flowers.

As they dart from flower to flower, bees and butterflies carry powdery **pollen** from one blossom to the next. Pollen is made by the male part of the flower. Tiny grains of pollen land on the **pistil**, the female part in the center of the flower. Then the flower begins to change. The petals fall away. The pistil swells as seeds form inside it.

Top: *This bumblebee is feeding on the nectar produced by the sunflower.*
Bottom: *A potato beetle eats the leaves of a potato plant.*

Insect Eaters

Insects that feed on garden plants may become meals themselves. Many animals come to the garden to hunt insects as **prey**. These hunters help to keep the number of plant-eating insects from getting too big, so insects do not eat all the plants.

Toads and lizards eat insects. Ladybug beetles catch small insects called **aphids**, which feed by sucking juices from plants. One ladybug may eat 5,000 aphids in its lifetime! Spiders catch many kinds of insects. Some spiders spin webs to catch their prey. The crab spider does not spin a web. It waits in a flower. When a bee or another insect lands on the flower, the spider attacks. It grabs the bee and eats it.

Top: Crab spiders wait for their prey on flowers. Bottom: A ladybug feeds on an aphid. By keeping the number of aphids low, ladybugs help the ecosystem.

Swarms of plant-eating Japanese beetles may visit a garden in summer.

Butterflies are among the most colorful of the insects that feed on flower nectar.

This toad sees a potato beetle. It is getting ready to catch and to eat the insect.

This anole lizard has come to the garden looking for insects to eat.

15

A Garden Life Story

An insect called the **praying mantis** sits with its front legs folded, as if it were praying. It is really waiting to pounce on prey! The mantis moves quickly, snatching an insect with its front legs.

The mantis lives its whole life in a garden. Young mantises **hatch** in spring and summer. The young mantises, called **nymphs**, begin to hunt for garden insects right away. They grow up to be adults that are from 3 to 4 inches (8–10 cm) long.

The female mantis lays her eggs in the garden in fall. She glues them to a twig with a sticky foam she makes with her body, and then she leaves them there.

Top Left: *Young mantises hatch from eggs in spring.* Center: *A female praying mantis lays her eggs in fall.* Bottom Left: *This adult praying mantis is about to strike its prey.*

The Slime Sisters

At night snails and **slugs** come out to feed on leaves, flowers, and berries. These animals make a slimy **mucus** that helps them to glide over the ground and the plants. In the morning, you may see the silvery trails of slime that they have left behind.

A slippery coating of mucus covers the earthworm, too. Earthworms tunnel through garden soil. They eat dirt, dead leaves, and other dead matter. When they **digest** these materials, the earthworms break them down into simple parts. The worms' waste is filled with nutrients. Garden plants take up the nutrients through their roots. In this way, worms help the garden to grow.

Top: *These three snails are feeding on a leaf.* Bottom: *Sweet fruits, such as strawberries, are food for slugs.*

Earthworms tunnel through the soil around the roots of plants, such as these radishes. The tunnels help air and water to reach the roots.

An earthworm pulls a leaf into the ground, where it will rot. Earthworms eat rotted leaves and other dead plant material. Their waste adds nutrients to the soil, helping the garden to grow.

21

Birds in the Garden

Some birds eat garden insects and worms. Other birds like seeds and berries. **Hummingbirds** feed on flower nectar. As do bees, hummingbirds carry pollen from flower to flower while they feed. Many hummingbirds eat small spiders, too.

Some birds raise their young in the garden. **Yellow warblers** build cup-shaped nests in the shelter of garden bushes. Yellow warblers line their nests with soft plant fibers. Then the female yellow warbler lays her eggs. The yellow warbler stays in the nest to keep the eggs warm until they hatch. Then she feeds and cares for the young until they are ready to fly. That happens about 12 days after they hatch. Yellow warblers eat insects. In this way, they help to protect the garden plants from insects.

Top: *As do bees, hummingbirds feed on nectar.* Bottom:*This yellow warbler will spend about 12 days keeping her eggs warm. Then the eggs will hatch.*

Furry Visitors

Small **mammals**, such as mice and **voles**, come to the garden in search of food. As the Sun rises or sets, you may see a rabbit feasting on leaves.

Chipmunks often make their homes in or near gardens. Chipmunks live in **burrows** under the ground. The burrows usually have several entrances, with long tunnels that the chipmunks dig. If the chipmunk senses danger, it dives into the closest tunnel.

Chipmunks and other small animals must be careful. **Predators** prowl the garden. One of the most dangerous predators in the garden is the house cat.

Top: *The garden is full of food for small mammals, such as this young white-footed mouse.* Bottom: *Rabbits like to visit the garden to snack on leaves.*

Voles are among the many animals that come to the garden to look for food. Voles are small mammals that are related to mice.

A house cat watches for mice, voles, and other small animals. Cats are garden predators.

Chipmunks dig burrows in or near gardens. Like voles, chipmunks like strawberries.

Into Everything

Raccoons usually sleep during the day and look for food at night, but sometimes they visit the garden in daylight. Raccoons eat almost anything, including garbage that people have put in trash cans. In a garden, they get into everything. Fruits, berries, birds' eggs, and insects are all tasty treats for a raccoon. Raccoons are especially fond of corn and other vegetables. They are good climbers and can easily get over a fence to reach the vegetable garden.

Raccoons have black fur around their eyes that looks like a mask. This makes raccoons look like bandits. To many gardeners, that is exactly what they are!

Top: *Raccoons have strong claws that they use to dig for insects and to open trash cans.* Bottom: *Gardeners put up fences to try to keep raccoons out.*

The Garden Community

All the living things that belong to this garden community depend on one another. The plants provide food for insects, such as bees and aphids, and for mammals, such as chipmunks and raccoons. Bees and hummingbirds help the plants to form seeds. Earthworms improve the soil to help the garden to grow. Some of the animals that eat plants become food for predators, such as the praying mantis and the house cat. Predators keep the plant eaters from eating all the plants.

As do the plants and the animals in a garden, living things everywhere depend on one another. A garden is just one of Earth's many small ecosystems.

Glossary

aphids (AY-fidz) Small insects that feed by sucking juices from plants.

buffet (buh-FAY) A meal laid out so that guests can serve themselves.

burrows (BUR-ohs) Holes that animals dig in the ground in which to live.

digest (dy-JEST) When a body breaks down food into energy.

ecosystem (EE-koh-sis-tem) A community of living things and the surroundings, such as air, soil, and water, in which they live.

hatch (HACH) To come out of an egg.

hummingbirds (HUH-ming-burdz) Small birds that feed on flower nectar.

mammals (MA-mulz) Animals that have hair and feed their young with milk from the mother's body.

mucus (MYOO-kus) A thick, slimy liquid produced by the bodies of many animals.

nectar (NEK-tur) A sugary liquid in the center of a flower.

nutrients (NOO-tree-ints) Anything that a living thing needs to live and to grow.

nymphs (NIMFS) The young of certain insects.

pistil (PIS-tuhl) The female part of a flower.

pollen (PAH-lin) A powder that comes from the male part of a flower.

praying mantis (PRAY-ing MAN-tis) A large insect that catches and eats other insects.

predators (PREH-duh-terz) Animals that catch and eat other animals.

prey (PRAY) An animal that is caught and eaten by another animal.

slugs (SLUHGZ) Animals that are like snails but have no shells.

voles (VOHLZ) Small animals that are members of the mouse family.

yellow warbler (YEH-loh WAR-blur) A songbird that eats insects and often nests in gardens.

Index

B
birds, 5, 23, 29
burrows, 24

E
ecosystem(s), 5, 30
eggs, 17, 23, 29

F
flower(s), 6, 11–12, 18

I
insects, 5–6, 12, 17, 23, 29–30

M
mammals, 24, 30
mucus, 18

N
nectar, 11, 23
nests, 23
nutrients, 6, 18
nymphs, 17

P
pistil, 11
pollen, 11, 23
predators, 24, 30
prey, 12, 17

R
raccoons, 29

S
soil, 5–6, 18, 30

Web Sites

Due to the changing nature of Internet links, PowerKids Press has developed an online list of Web sites related to the subject of this book. This site is updated regularly. Please use this link to access the list:
www.powerkidslinks.com/lse/gardeco/